FREEDOM of FAITH

G B BERNHARDS

Copyright @2021 by G B Bernhards

All rights reserved. No part of this book may be reproduced in any form or by any electronic or mechanical means, including information storage and retrieval systems, without permission in writing from the publisher, except by reviewers, who may quote brief passages in a review.

This publication contains the opinions and ideas of its author. It is intended to provide helpful and informative material on the subjects addressed in the publication. The author and publisher specifically disclaim all responsibility for any liability, loss or risk, personal or otherwise, which is incurred as a consequence, directly or indirectly, of the use and application of any of the contents of this book.

WORKBOOK PRESS LLC
187 E Warm Springs Rd,
Suite B285, Las Vegas, NV 89119, USA

Website:	https://workbookpress.com/
Hotline:	1-888-818-4856
Email:	admin@workbookpress.com

Ordering Information:
Quantity sales. Special discounts are available on quantity purchases by corporations, associations, and others.
For details, contact the publisher at the address above.

Library of Congress Control Number:
ISBN-13:   978-1-956876-24-6 (Paperback Version)
            978-1-956876-25-3 (Digital Version)

REV. DATE: 10/11/2021

FREEDOM OF FAITH

By
G B Bernhards

How Many Dots

How many have you made

That God Could say

You made a dot for me.

How many have you made

That others could say

You made a dot for me.

In the end God will count all

The dots you made for him and

How you lived your life with him.

Your Song

Somewhere you are

Somehow you feel

Somewhere you will find me

Somehow I ask you for peace

Sometime you will understand

Sometime you will realize

Somehow I will remain

So now I ask you to stay.

So Sweet

I watched you make

Our sandwiches,

I laughed in my mind.

I laughed for you

Were so sweet

Trying your best

To please me.

I would like to hear

your voice, once more,

Touch you, hold you,

And smile in my heart.

RIP JOE 29-08-1973

DIED 17-02-1987

WITH US

May God be with us

May the blessing survive

May love never be denied

May we choose to be reborn

With all the love

We have hidden inside

Then we will survive

With all our love and

With dignity for all life.

To Remain

I don't understand

As a human how

The world I am in

Survives and hopefully

Stays that way I do not like to judge

Them anymore I like to be a friend

To all those who still believe

That some humans are kind

And do not remain blind

And want to live in peace.

TO THE LORD

To the Lord

Who loves and heals

Who feels and gives

Us love

To the Lord

Who loves and keeps

Who wins and weeps

For us

TO WAIT

With time and caring

We share one another

With trust and love

We have one another

So, let us bring joy

And love to the world

That wait for peace

And happiness.

Time brings belief

To this world

Who is hoping for

A place with you

Where you are

Lord, we pray to thee

May the world have

Joy in sharing time together

With or without me.

Too Blind to See

Lord you gave me so much

Which, I didn't take

Lord you said so much

Which I didn't hear.

Thank you lord

Don't give up on me

Thank you for the happiness

I have had, I hope I can bring it all back.

This world is full of people

Who need you

They only have to see and hear once more

What you did for them and me.

And now it is the time to thank you Jesus

For all the love and caring

Thank you Jesus for all the good

That you have done

Thank you Jesus for the peace

That will come when the world will be one

Caring for their brothers and sisters

Like we all belong in paradise with God.

The Measure of Value

Jesus I am worthy to be

wasted some time on

I'll do what I think you want

I will keep going on

I know I don't love you

As much as you deserve

I can feel your love

Growing in my world

I want to see you in the sky

If my eyes don't fool me

I'll see you in the light

Then the night will hide

I long to hear you say once again

Freedom of Faith

You will forget your pain

Keep your belief in me

Believe in love again

I feel like I am hunted

By my past

Hasn't left me

The way of the dark

Is someone who wants

Your words to be a lie

I don't pity Satan

In my world he tries

To turn us to his hell

With his spell attempts and pain

To destroy true love

How weak we are to give to him

Who fight the king of love

How stupid are we to think

That true love can be a sin

I know you will come to me
I hope that day will come but
I might be gone for
I might have lost myself

Inside me is a strong will
To be strong like you
Live forever and to win
False, temptations and weaknesses

I pray for the future
I hope many will hear
Your words of truth
Like you have said

Care for your brother
Love one another
I say there is a need

To care for one another

Who will dare to measure
Themselves to thee my Lord
Who will be tempted to think
I am better off without your words

My Lord Jesus

He is the son of God

In him I believe

I shall conquer myself

I might not be able to

Sing for the crowd

But I hope someone will

Hear me out loud

When I scream out into the night

Your words and in fright

I could make them think of you

Instead of themselves

How lonely many are

Living like clocks on the wall

Waiting for someone

To make them go on

My mind is up I am not

Turning my back on you

I hopefully will learn to

Behold you in my world

Hear me know come to see

At your own face in the mirror

Do you have something to hide

You should not hide from God

I would live where he places me,

I would take what he offered me

I would give what he wanted me to give

I would say what he wanted me to say

I long for a tomorrow

For tomorrow is the day

Shorter for me to get to heaven

Live by his side as a child again

The Happy Happenings

The new world is growing

Showing us that we can

Live it through with our children

The new hope is coming

Something we could be given

Hope to be like children again

Through our life's

With a style

We will enter again

To help those who

Need to feel the

Power of caring

That God is

Helping us

He will find us.

The Help

I would like to sing the songs

Who would join us together

Who would stay with us forever

In love—in love

So long—so fine

With love we might find

Loves joining us like a prayer

Could I sing

A love song all day long

Like when I first kissed

Saved my pride

So lost—so in love

Is the best thing that

Happened to me

True, true love

For someone to be

Like you and me

Lonely like me

We share and we are

Grateful for today

Thank you Lord for helping me.

The Holy Light

Holy your light has

Shined like a star

In the sky to me.

I have not repented for long

But I can share with you

The hope of the glory

And behold, then I will see you.

I want to learn more

About the light

Who is here and there

And the hope for evermore.

To share with us

To be with us like the stars

To be like a sister

To be like a lovely child.

The Humble One

I feel shy and embarrassed

In the crowd

I rather like to climb a mountain

And to sing for you for a hole day or two

About the love we have for others

About the time we share together

That might be forever

To prepare us for him.

The Day After

Still is the air

Cool is the night

Temptations are to try

To make me fall into

A nervous breakdown

I will not be happy

Without your trust

Time will change

With your glory

Cause the entire world might

Sing a song of mine

I wrote for you

To tell them that

You are and you care

Love never dies

When we are your children

You will remember us

Within our time

in faith in you we remain yours

And you surrender us from evil.

THE DEFEATED ONE

Please don't let them

Take what you got

Please don't let them

Take what you look

Please don't let them

Take away your belief.

The Dessert

I am but a grain of sand

In the desert

Not a burning bush

Respect one another

Care for one another

Love one another

It is time to think of

Redemsion and religion

And repentance, repent

Among us are flowers

We cannot tell

Their difference between

Their colors

Like everyone else are

Like anyone else we feel

Keep up being believers

G B Bernhards

Don't let the shade

Of darkness blind you

Believe in the Lord.

THE DESPERATE ONES

Now this is my time

To make a sign

I have declared

Every souls right

My tongue talks

Evil words and lies

No one can be

As much as a sinner

No heart can be

In deeper darkness

But still there is a hope

That heaven stays above

I thank the few who

Told me story's

Story's about the light

Hidden inside

Story's that made the child's eyes

Grow wide and lively again

The word of life is power

That keeps you strong

I thank the Lord for the

Love he has shown

Hope my way of life

Will change into the right

Colors of the light

Where will I go after love

If it isn't already here

Where will I seek the truth

If it isn't in me

Why must temptations

Appear on our days.

Can't we stand side by side

Shutting down the nonsense

I can't be a judge for I feel

Pity for the sinner

I can't be anything else but me

The young winner

Who is also a sinner

The Development of Life

Met a girl who was my friend

I wondered how naïve

She still were

We talked about nothing

And I was thinking

What to say

I knew that she hadn't

Changed her lifestyle

And took no chances

I felt like she was

A coward not willing to

And took no chances

I felt like she was

A coward not willing to

Take any risks

I knew how much better

I felt after changing

My lifestyle I felt like she wouldn't

Realize how much better

Things could become

I don't envy her

I feel sorry for her

For she thinks the same

As many years ago

It's like her mind does not

Keep on growing

Thinking differently

I'm glad for I know I have changed.

II

When I look into some

People's eyes

I feel hurt inside

Many people are neither

Happy or unhappy

At the bus one morning

I noticed in the crowd

A nice young face

with heartbroken eyes

I was unhappy and for some time

I did not know happiness at all

I hope few of us were like me

The memory of that face

Stays in my mind for it

Reminds me of the face

Who once could have been mine

The chosen few are not

Worrying about us

But we know how hard it is

To be living it all.

The Difference of a Prayer

I am sitting on the floor

with a book in my hand

Singing poems to myself

Listening to my voice

When I sing the words of

Prayers in my mind

I saw myself standing

on a hill singing

for the world

Is it all a dream

Or real

Do you dream

That you are different

From the rest

In some way

THE DOUBT

Have mercy on me Lord

For I have sinned

I feel like I have let you down

Somewhere within

I want to know you Lord

You are the truth

So I can love you more

You are my light

I feel unworthy for you

I want to repent to you

With the words I sing within

For once I want my dreams to come true

I would sing for you hoping

You would forgive me

For I have sinned

Thank you I say with all my heart

I believe you will let me find

My true love within myself

Then I know where to find

Love for another person

Lord thank you for not

Forgetting about me

I am one of your lost sheep

I hope you can get me back

I have changed my life

I wanted to find my way back

I wanted you to hear me

Like a child again I sing for thee

I thought what could I do for you

Felt so small and so weak

For I haven't done enough for you

You showed me the way to my heart

Like a child I live for you

Like a child I sing for you

Like a child I am happy too

Like the love I have for you.

The Dream

I have a dream

Of being one of the

Flowers in your garden

I have a dream

of being one of the

Running wild deer

In the garden of peace

Where there are no children

with fear

I love to walk in the park

Dreaming of you

In a child's way again

That once I wanted to be small

in your arms and

Feeling safe.

The End

Oh, Lord you are

My shelter and my friend

Oh, Lord you are

My hope and when I can

I will look upon your face

I will see the eyes who

Love without an end.

You taught me with

Your words

I believe my life will be

Without an end

For I love you

Believe in you

And no life ends with death.

The Fear to be Lost

Please don't take away

My belief in the

King of light

There will be no night

In my life when I believe

I could go to live in heaven

He is the forgiveness

He is the son of the true God

Who we believe in and learn how to trust.

The Future

Why am I to be

So happy to see

My life in a new light

It makes me happy

That I have been in thought

of my Lord

I know maybe

He will

Listen to me.

The Guardian

I feel the nearness

I feel the clearness

Of the lord in my life

I feel the future

I feel the nature

In my soul

I feel the sorrow

I feel tomorrow

I'll be on my way

I feel the nearness

I feel the clearness

I feel downhearted

I feel departed

from you my friend

I'm a puzzle

You absolutely

Have to solve

I feel the nearness

I feel the clearness

Of my Lord

Near the path of truth

Stand old strong trees

I believe in the truth

We all see a star

Brightest of them all

We know the path is long

We must try to be strong

to love we belong.

The Appearance of the Lord in my Life

When I look up in the sky

I wonder why

I ask me how

It's all begun

When I see you each day

I feel happy

I ask me why

You make me glad

When I feel the rain

on my face

I ask me how

If comes and goes

When I write things down,

I wonder why

I ask myself

why it seems natural

The Baby Girl

God has the power of love

We easily walk into
Temptation and sorrow
He tries to comfort us and
Care like we are children

He is the ruler of all life
Who he hopes will be his in the end
For I will tell them
That God is an everlasting Lord

As children we might have seen God
Someone taught me this language
That's why I sing for you in my mind
So you will have a memory of me.

The Bad Excuse for Violence

I don't want to be your second best

I want to be with you in your test

We can together

You could alone

But maybe better

If I help along

We could sing and dance

Bring joy to this world

Clean the dirt away

with our tears

Our souls are looking

For the truth

The truth that's in us all

We like to know

A prayer is important

We believe in everything good

Not in anger and revenge.

The Bad Prayer

This morning is like death

Quite as a grave

I feel I'm losing life

Now I am hearing a death rattle

Dreamed I was a decoy

Walking down the stairs

Made me fear

Made me share

The fright of death

Nevertheless

I saw the gosts' ride

Black horses

I ran but didn't get far

They came in front of me

They came behind me

One of them walked to me

He had golden eyes

I asked if they were coming for me

He said I give you a chance

I'm coming for you again

When the leaves fall down

When the cold wind blows

You will die

I thought, so little time left

I have to walk on the mountain again

Catch fish in the water before I go

Nevertheless, I will die one day

The Church

Imagine what Maria

Did for us to give us

Our holy belief in the Lord

Imagine how the sun

Brightens our earth

Holy light is brighter

Imagine what his love

Did for us in his name

And from his story's.

The Confessions of a Girl

You are to be free

Like the soul inside of me

You are to be holy within

They whisper to thee

Sunshine shines on me

Give me the love you keep

I would be yours till eternity

If I had my life with thee

Strange to hear the singing

Beautiful to see you move

It gives me strength

to continue with my life

See you flying in the air

and the hope we share

for with time we will see

Heaven is for those who keep

To keep their belief

Love and honesty

Saved me away

I would stay

For I need love to see you in my mind

And to be free in my heart

For you live with me already

In my soul and in my blood

The one to be with your child

Rich of all the children

We can later be with the blessed

For we will still be up there

We could do something together

Like swimming in the air

We could do everything for one another

Like saving one more soul for heaven

Loves still grows on and

We will be saved

With our lifestyle's

We have made.

The Conscience

I hear you calling

I fear you're hulling

I care for you

I need to hear from you

I don't see clearly

I don't know what I need

I don't know as you

I need to know more to know why

Tell me truly am I to be somebody

Who could be of use in a fight?

Who could be of use to the light?

I hear somebody needing

I feel somebody pleading

I feel someone kneeling

Does he really love me too

I see his eyes in my mind

I feel he wants to reach out to me

I feel he heals my soul

I know he has a goal

II

You are so far away

Still we see the same sun

We are so far apart

Still we see the same moonlight

What do I feel?

I'm so confused

What do I need?

I'm so robbed of you

G B Bernhards

I was almost there

To reach for you

I'm longing to hear

The truth from you

Am I one of those?

Who never can choose

Between good and bad

So afraid to lose.

SHINE THE LIGHT

Like the light

That shines

Inside your soul

That's your goal

To keep it shining

And feeling love

And understanding

It's not for all

Time will tell

Until then

Keep the faith

And believe in love

For the Lord is love

He looks at us

Then he sees

Only his children

Fear not the past

Try today to

Live everyday

At your best

Who will know

What tomorrow

Has for us to share

Do we even care

II

We are all children to him

No matter what

How do you think of God?

He would not put anyone bad into a baby

We are all unwritten pages

An empty book

We write our own lives

as we live day by day

Look at your life as a holiday

Because forever is a longtime

Trust in yourself

You are neither better nor worse

Then any other people out there.

Spirits are Coming

I feel the spirits coming closer

I hope they want me well

I feel like a sick personality

I am not sure if I can fight them back

I was a dog-tired as I laid myself down,

I woke up tired and pleased

I felt pleased that I was not forgotten

I thought I knew what I wanted

I phoned him, he came again

Humbled as usual, not too proud

He came as a friend but

When he left, he was a man

I told you my secrets

Freedom of Faith

I told you why I left

I told you so you would understand

That I was not myself

My inner person has fought a war

My inner person is I

But I was too shy to be myself

For I didn't know how to be proud

I feel in love today

With another man

My inner person knows why

I did not say goodbye

I know as I look into your eyes

God must have brought us together

and no man may break us apart

for after all you were mine

I shivered inside

What was wrong

Why did I risk everything

Just to keep your love

I have to go for a visit

I don't want to waste my time

I arrived to soon, so I went for a walk

Alone in my hometown

There I was walking

Not having any place to go

There I heard you call out to me

I felt the presence of your soul

My friend you have gone away

You died so suddenly

I didn't try to say goodbye

For I believed in another life

I heard you my friend

As I stand by your grave

Your whisper makes me feel good again

But I can't understand what you are

trying to say

I walked a long way

To visit your grave,

I did not realize where I was going

Until I saw the hill

The hill where the house of God stands

Near the place where you rest your bones

In the garden of the dead

I believe our souls grow elsewhere

I was afraid to go near your grave

But I thought about Jesus

Talking and thinking over his life

I felt my true love for Jesus

I hoped you were sent from him

to tell me something or to warn me

I remember thinking that at last

I did the right thing

I felt like a mother carrying her child

A child who was just a day old

I felt the nearness of my child

As I grew like a part of me

I thought I couldn't do anything this time

and felt tired and frightened

That I wouldn't have the time

To do anything for myself.

Sunshine

It's felt like the sunshine

Is in my soul

My love for you

When I write about my

Faith in you

I am a five-year-old

Baby girl again

Like a child of innocence

I look up to you and see

that I can trust you

And that I do

I am a baby girl

Playing on the beach

Like someone's showing me

We are all the same

to start with in our life's

Innocence is something

That is wrong to take away

for we were all children

and all the same

What we say or do

To one another is hell

Must get those bad feelings

Of anger away

Please forgive me but

Should they all be forgiven

Jesus Forever

Jesus I am trying to be

Like you

Give me a second chance

Jesus I am a fool

I don't know you too well

But I believe in you

Jesus tell me

Should I leave him

But I think I love him

Jesus tell me

Should I carry on

To be his best friend

G B Bernhards

Jesus tell me

Should I never try to

Have any children

Jesus don't you

Love all men

Then I can be with him

Jesus don't you

Treat every man?

Aren't we all equal?

Jesus don't you believe me

I want well

I want to be better

Jesus I am afraid

Do you notice me?

Do you accept me?

Jesus I am a fool

I don't know you too well

But I believe in you

Jesus, in Your Garden

Jesus, I haven't done enough

Forgive me please

Jesus, I haven't prayed enough

Please have mercy on me

Jesus tell me is it true

Will I die soon

Jesus I want to be with you

But I am not worthy

Why do I feel so sad

Made me scared

I don't know much, I'm not wise

Please can I be

The only thing I need to know

Is your philosophy.

Jesus, Put My Soul

Jesus put me

With your flowers

In your garden

Jesus put my soul

In your garden

Where you grow

Your souls

Jesus place me

Where you want me to be

I know there are no

Evils plants in your garden

II

Jesus don't leave me

Am I not one of

Your lost sheep

Sheppard take care

I don't want Evil

To come near

I know how bad it can

Be in our lives

I don't doubt your power

Jesus I believe in you

Jesus, with Your Flowers

Jesus, I want to drink

Your cup of blood

Jesus, I want to taste

Your piece of bread

Mormons tell me I can't with them

For I am protestant

Jesus can you tell me

Who is wrong me or them

I think every man has a right

To have the sacrament

I think every man needs to

Be cleaned inside out

Can you tell me?

What is wrong?

Why I am afraid?

Jesus

Jesus when I die

I might die tomorrow

Or after hundred years

Jesus I want you to

Save my soul

Take my soul

For I love you

I don't love you

The why I should do

I don't know how

I am to love you

I close my eyes

To the hell in me

Freedom of Faith

I don't want to die

I don't want to go to hell

I don't want to die

I am praying to you

Please take my soul to heaven

I might die tomorrow

or after a hundred years

I wash my face

In my tears

That I cry

I carry a little cross

In a chain

My soul carried

A bigger cross

My mind is in

The dark

My hope is in

The light

I wish I could get

The little devil

Out of my heart

My heart is poisoned

The mad little devil

Is always putting

In words I hate

I wish I could get

You're the king

Into my heart

My inner man cries

For you Jesus

My inner man hungers

For you Jesus

Words like my Lord

When I want to say

Dear Lord

Mad little devil in me

Seems out of place

I want to throw him out

Jesus save my soul

I might die tomorrow

or after hundred years

Like to be

Somewhere I am

Somewhere you are

Somewhere we are waiting

To be together again

Together we will see

The light of heaven

To see the sky of forever

To explore the secrets

Together again

With hope to be able

To stay together

Like the comfort of a prayer

MARIA

Love for the woman

Who was so noble to me

The mother of a man

Who freed us from slavery

Glory to her memory

She was chosen to

Give life to the king

Of love and light

To whom we share our love

And sorrow with

She was so innocent

She understood

the responsibility about

Bringing him up for us

She will be the lady

For the women

With her lifestyle of

Honesty and innocence

And with her true love for us.

My Trust in You

To my life

you are more than a song

To my life

you are more than a poem

You are a legend

That will last

You are a friend

I like the best

I felt when I was very young

I saw you in my mind and

You thought me how

The way to sing and dance

Also to love mentally

All humanity.

Note to Evil is Out!

If you are into evil

You decide for yourselves

If you want to live

Or if you want to die

No soul deserves the darkness

Nobody wants to go to him

We disconnect the body

and the soul with their DNA

Oblivion is the darkness

For the darkness is nothing

And nothing after is

Dust to dust

So, pray that you may be

In your body or your soul

For otherwise you are lost

And we don't hear your cry

For a dead DNA does not

Sound from the grave

It is the end

Alfa and Omega is not a human

So let's pray for our souls

For a soul is not lost

Just the capsule around it

For no soul is born dead.

Hallelujah

Hallelujah

I do believe

I believe in him

There is something

in the air

Love is back to stay

in him I trust

There is something

They're for me to see

In the Lord I must trust

Hope for humanity

Is always here

but they must beware

Of their own shade of doubt

Nature take its course

We live in reality but

There is something else out there

God does not hope

or want us to be hurt or die

Its nature and life

For God is love

I Love You

You smile with your eyes

and sorrow goes away

You smile to me

You say

I love you,

I love you

So many years have gone by

But still you come

When I feel down

Then you sing to me I love you

You say, 'Take good care of my brothers.

They are so young.

Tell them I love them and miss them

They don't see me anymore'

I say, 'I miss you, I love you,

You, my prettiest one.'

I was Surprised

I lost a friend today,

She thought I was somebody else.

I lost a frightening teacher,

She thought me about a dangerous race.

I hope she will become normal

As I talked about feelings of love,

she took that for a judgement

I am not a judger at all.

I think marriage is next to God

And children his joy

I love my family though

Problem might get too rough.

I don't think dirty about sex

It's wonderful when you love someone.

I like to be left alone

with my time and place at least

A couple of years of peace and joy.

IMMANUEL

May your glory shine

May your heart be divine

Love is for everyone

For in kingdom come

May we all learn to

Help someone.

May we all sing

A song or two

For it is Christmas.

We hopefully have joy

But at least we

Have one another.

IMMANUEL IS HOPE

For you,

there is a kingdom of light.

For you have conquered yourself

towards light.

We are with you

After we arrived.

Then you will pray and stay

We are your big family.

There is always someone waiting for you.

To show you the light in yourself.

Who will survive with us, So with no fright

We stay in the light.

Love has arrived here to us

Love is to share with us.

There is hope for everyone before God

If we are honest and sincere to him.

When I touch your hand

It will give me strength

To carry on with my song

With my life as a prayer.

IN TIME

Time is what we share

Love is that we care

Time will let us be

Together again.

HOLY ANGEL

Why don't you leave me alone?

You're wasting your time?

I am not worthy for you.

Good spirits you are holy

I am only shading your work

You have on me

In my heart, I am failure

In my soul, I am fooling myself.

In my inner person, there is hope.

I feel your love for me

And I feel sick to have let you down.

Am I to give up on myself?

Or should I keep on?

The answer is not difficult,

But will I answer?

Hope

The time came

when I needed strength and self-respect.

After I thought dark thoughts

And was with anger.

Lord helps me to get over this

Lord let me think of hope

Of love

I might want to have.

I share my thoughts of you

with many souls.

I share my fright of you

with someone else.

Lord I need to be good.

Lord I need to plead to you.

Thank you for the good you brought me

For I dreamed I wanted to have a life.

II

I hope I can call your name

And let everyone hear,

How good you are to us.

We should thank you

For what you gave us.

We thank you for our lives

We hope to be able

To grow ourselves

Into a community of you

I Don't Live Just To

I don't live just to buy paintings

I don't live just to buy food

I don't live just for my parents

I live for you

I live the life you wanted me too

We are so wrong

Changing all the tunes

The tunes you have made

For us to hear.

We are so wrong

Destroying our lives.

The life you have given

Us to live, us to love.

We are so wrong

Telling people words of truth,

Truth which people have changed into lies

The words were too difficult for them,

To change their lifestyle

So long good sailor, so long good farmer,

So long good driver, so long good wife

So long good youth,

So long.

So long, men are changing everything

Into hell, hell, hell

We are not supposed to dream anymore

We are not supposed to live anymore

We are not supposed to love anymore

We are not supposed to think anymore.

We are not supposed to give and take

We are not supposed to sleep or work

We are not supposed to eat,

or have fun in any way.

We are turning into robots

We are turning into steal ammunition.

Is the true word and money is our faith?

The Lord is a forgotten freedom.

Now people of the world are in hell

And only God can save us.

We want to change

We can if we try.

Everyone can

just by start thinking in another way

Start by being human,

Human with feelings

Truth and love.

God moves in mysteries ways.

*Does it not feel bad to know
That you haven't done enough?
Does it not feel good to know,
that you have started it now.*

*Our Lord is the only,
Only one Lord in this world.
We better get started
to know.*

*That he moves in mysteries ways
That he loves every man
That he wants us all to be free
It is only the way we live that blind us.*

*We are no better than the rest,
and the rest
is no better than the others.*

It seems like it's all a test.

Mother you are blinded.

You wanted me to be like you.

Father you are blinded.

You wanted me to be your loving child.

How can a child show love?

If it hasn't known, it before

How can a child live?

When the parents are creating a hell,

Not a home.

I love you mother

I love you father

We are all sick in our way.

Mother,

uncountable men have laid with you

Father,

uncountable bottles have stayed with you.

I am telling you,

so you can beware

Of the false,

and the bad things in life.

Mother I am glad you brought me up

but you would never have made me a man

Father I am glad you stayed out

You might have made me worse than I am

The Lord made my life change

The Lord heard my prayers

I was naive full of wrong things I couldn't help it,

it was the only thing I ever saw.

II

Two men came my way

They both look alike.

The first time I saw them,

I realized a light.

A light I never saw before

Light came into my life.

Days passed and years went

My friends made me a person of skill

And belief of will and kindness

So I am forgetting the easy life

By starting to be different

Than those who are living as ill

The stranger speaks loudly to me

Shove it, shove it

up into yours

Just blow it, just blow it

out to hell

My home is a hell

Hell is where I am living

Don't mess with me buster

I am the big man around.

I know about everything

From the rats to pimps, all the way to the pigs.

Just don't cause any trouble,

Or you might die tonight.

I was afraid of the anger in his face

Why do you talk so badly to me?

Why do you talk such quality?

Don't you listen anymore to love and respectful things?

I know the system is false, abusing us

But if we make a revolution,

Others would not accept that

and start another.

We could be in chain of troubles,

deeper troubles than now

Don't you see why?

I say look at the people

who are not thinking.

People who don't think themselves

People who don't take parts in anything

But to please themselves.

The angry man "my life is shit"

I answer, "That is why you treat it that way"

The angry man "my home is bad"

I answer, "That's because you don't want one"

He again "my life is in the gutter man"

I more affectionate "if you think of your life that way

It only shows others how little you appreciate your life"

"If you live as shit you may have caused it

I can't believe you get born in the gutter"

He almost crying, "I was, just ask my mom,

she lives in the house with the pimps"

I almost desperate "how can that be,

how did it all start?

Are people not trying to get away from the dark?

Can someone not help those?

Who wants help?

Why do people listen to

stupid things in the streets?

Why do people

say stupid things in the heat?

Isn't life going backwards?

Isn't man destroying the humanity?

In the few of us that are left,

Who try to think in a nice way of people nowadays?

Many people talk about me.

Many of them badly

I feel sorry for them

For they see something in me

That is missing in them

If not, they wouldn't have noticed me.

I dress like thousands others

Still you know me

I walk like many others

Still you stare at me.

Why is something wrong?

In what way am I different to you?

The crowd you walk

like you got heaven under your feet

You look into the crowd

Not afraid of anyone.

He answers,

Yes, I am afraid

Some people would like to hurt me

Kill me, if they could.

You can't think the way you want to
You can't say the things you need to
You can't be yourself in a country
Where people don't know themselves.

No goal in life, how?
If you don't life for something,
You only live for yourself.
If you like living, it will show.
If you don't,
then it's called Self-destruction or torture,
we might all be masochists
That's better than being dead.

God Is

The world is in love

The World is temptation

The world is weak and bright

The world is strong and dark.

For we say we believe

For we read the book

For we judge others badly

For we will be judged by you.

I love you

like a bird that is free

I love you

like a strong tree

I love you

like I am still a baby.

Maybe with time we will be

Able to be with love

And in belief in the Lord

We could explore heaven.

A Hidden Secret Hid

A hidden secret

hid on a mountain top

For you to find,

It might change your mind.

The mountain is surrounded

by big cliffs

Almost no way there

but something's in the air.

I stare down

at the valley beneath me.

I hear a voice singing to me

Pray to me, pray to me

Then I decided to be

In eternity for that world

Is more to me

than You and me.

A Touch of Innocence

A girl denies God

For she has suffered

A child in intense

To believe in love

And can only learn

to make those demands

Go to waste.

You hurt a soul

than that soul is marked

for future to come

You can change the wound,

into a well of wisdom

If you place your heart

in the arms of a friend.

She went into a way of punishing herself

She builds a wall of ignorance

She only made the demands

Who would go to waste

You hurt a soul, you mark it for life

Forgiveness can make the pain go away

But the wound stays with her

For what's left of her future.

A Baby Again

Jesus Christ,

you love me?

I love you

Where I am to be

You don't want to tell me

I have to find that out myself

Have mercy for me

For I am a child

Who is hardly grown up

To take care.

Forgive me

For the things I have done

Thought and said

You know what is mine.

I can hardly find out

What belongs to me.

I can't wait to see you,

And I look Forward to.

I am trying

to picture you in my mind.

What do you look like?

Because I Am

One thing

I will never give away

One thing

I will never change

The only thought that kept me sane

was 'Would I ever be found

By you, who I believe in'

By you, who I breathe for.

I thank you today

That no matter what you God

You don't give up on your children

For we are all your children

Born with the same gift

To be able to breathe

and The will to love you

Then nature takes its course.

Believe It or Don't

I believe today

that You were sent to me

to teach me

the truth of you.

You did not judge me

You were kind

and gave me

some of your time.

I would have doubted you

and your mission

if I Hadn't been guided again.

The message was to receive

And obey doubtlessly

What you had to say.

In my spirit

I was surprised

Conclusion was on my side

God bless you for showing me how.

Today I pray

and beg for strength

For I consider tomorrow

I might be sanctimonious.

I regained my hope

and my dreams

I'm not forgotten as I thought

He has showed me, I am not.

Brothers in Belief

You are so far away

But I feel so close to you

You are so far away

But I feel so near to you

You are a man

Don't despair.

We will be joined

Together in souls

We will be together

In our future to come.

For we were together

Before we got born

Like brothers and sisters

We have our eternal love.

DEAR LORD

Black

You changed my life

Made it so real

Now you left me to reality

Who am I?

I know what I want

Who am I?

I know what I need

Am I dreaming?

Are you gone?

White

You still love me

You make me happy

I find my comfort in you

I will get as much love I need

From where love was born

Lord you are not far away

I need your caring

I trust you

You love me for who I am

Who am I?

Did You Tell Me?

I don't want you to come here
If you've been thinking that again
He will be here the rest of the day
He would just read your mind
I don't want him to feel unhappy
I know I heard myself say
As I rushed to the door.

Now I just thought
What a sweet free innocent child
Does love and peace grow with him
You have chosen the hardest way
Reality is near where is your happiness
Unfair misjudges look at yourselves
Am I any worse than you are.

EVERYTIME I SING

Everytime I sing, I pray

With my singing I please my soul

Knowing I am pleasing my Lord

Who sends the spirits to keep me going on.

When I write my songs

I feel the power in my soul

I can do anything I want

Now that I am living to please myself.

Evil Mirror Goes Away

I had a long walk

I had a long talk

with my mirror

I bought it the other day

and it's new and bright

Shows my eyes in another light.

I was looking in the mirror yesterday

I saw my face and thought "it's me!"

Tonight, I looked into my eyes.

How can a soul be shy too its body?

I never dared staring at myself

Now I am trying not to hide from myself.

Evil has owned my body and heart

Kindness has taken that away

For my soul had a long talk.

Two eyes in the mirror

One sick, the others not

My attention was always with the sick one.

Tonight, I first sang me a song

I was too strong to lose

I no longer cared only for the sick one.

Belief is stronger than doubt

but doubt is strong for I feel

Evil does not want to lose me.

Tonight, in the mirror

I saw how black deep and pure

the stone was in the eye of my inner person.

Tonight, in the mirror

I saw how black my life had been

My soul was in no games.

Tonight, in the mirror

I saw how black false and nasty

the rock in the eye of my body.

To think that you look in the mirror

Just to see your face

Is no grace

but to ask and too please your soul.

I felt angry ashamed

Evil had its home in me

Now I was throwing them all out.

To think that a long walk in the rain

Hurts your body not your soul

and opens up your mind towards yourself.

EXIT

Spirits have left me behind

or have I closed my door

Right on their faces.

I have misunderstood their aim

I took control to soon

And I was left out.

I misused my skill

The skill I have learned

by being a believer.

I believe I am an idealist

I believe that Jesus wants me to be honest

But I am too stupid to confess.

Too know, what is knowing

Aren't we learning every day?

Aren't we caring too much for ourselves?

You tried to warn me

My dear friend

I misunderstood your message.

When will I grow up?

When will I know

When my man comes along?

Would I fall in love?

Would I forgive?

Could I be forgiven?

Soon It will be all over

Soon I look back and wonder

Soon I will learn to see my past without a measure

Soon I will find what it is to be myself.

Myself is always laughing

and others won't see

That I am not unhappy, but not happy either.

Ordinary me is like everyone else

No one would believe that

Ordinary me might become

Something different then they are.

Found Friendship

Black hair and brown eyes

I love you

So small and so crazy

I know you.

You told me

You want to go

Where God

and the Children are, you know.

I worried so much somehow

and asked you to stay

Somehow, I went crazy

Never knowing if you would try to go.

Today I feel like yesterday scared

Afraid to lose you

I truly love you

As you know.

We had the same a like spirits

But nights were so long

The last candle burned out

Were we here all alone?

We were cold and hungry

But he drank it all

So no wonder I got crazy

Now I am always lazy.

And nights were so long

Help me God to carry on

Heaven hold us, don't let go

Heaven can tell you, what I know.

So sweet so friendly

So much weep

Missing you cut me deep

But I try to hold on.

I did not understand

What had gone into you

So friendly and sweet

Also looking good for me.

Our Time

I

One day I thought

I was smart

and Well educated.

Day after I thought

I was naive and still

A lot left to learn.

Today I don't measure

Myself to anyone

For my life is different

From others

I look out for greed

And beware to think

That I am any better

Than others are.

On the contrary I have

Been considered

Weak and unsuccessful.

One day I thought

The Children I have

Had already left.

One day I thought

No matter what

I still have God

And my belief.

II

Happy family life is natural

If you are alone and feeling sad

You might need a family to care for.

Too many are fooling themselves

by living alone, they think

They are happier

Only caring for themselves.

I have some day's lost patience

I have some day's gone mad

but there are a lot more days'

I was happy and grateful.

To have a friend who you

Wake up with every morning

Be awake with every evening

You feel glad to have a friend.

To have a husband who you
Care for and cook with every day
Who you spend Sundays' with
You feel like you are needed.

To have a lover who you
Hold in your arms
and talk to in the night
Words of feeling and future.

To have a dream who you
Make appear in yourself
When you need comfort or understanding
When there is none at all, then I dream.

To have a child who you like to
Give all you're love to and

Patience is a main rule and then you

Understand, what it is all for

And why you are a child for God.

To have the Lord live with you

to think of and pray to

When you quit needing something

To make you feel grateful.

To have memories

You hold them in sight

Don't take them into the light

They mostly turn to be shadows.

MADNESS

Have you tried to look into a hungry child's eyes?

Have you tried to touch its bony body?

Can you imagine that child as yours?

Can you imagine that child as you?

How many days will the little child suffer?

How many nights must it feel death come closer?

Have you ever touched a baby dead body?

Have you ever held one in your arms?

It lies on the face of the earth, alone

It has no mother, has no home

It has no food, has no love

It has a reason to live, but how.

When a child dies one feel guilt

Dying is frightening, but quilt is painful

When a hungry child has died

It's found more heaven

Than we ever could find.

Has one not said to care for your brother?

So why do we build earth so selfishly?

Have people not said words to wake up others?

So why don't we all give, a little love.

(1981)

THE GREATEST OF ALL

O Lord, you gave us your life

And all your love,

Holy is your name.

So don't be angry with me Lord

For I have this dream to get the chance

To call out your name.

Jesus, Jesus.

You are the only light that is true

and what you went through

In your life Lord.

Were we worth the pain, you felt them?

Were we worth the gain, you had then?

Glory to you, you have for us given so much.

I believe in you Jesus, Jesus.

I don't need a sign to believe.

So, for you all who want to hear

Glory to you all who believe.

He is with us till the end

and in belief we up rise

Towards the light.

Marriage as a Combine

Today I give you my blessings

Today I give you a present

Today I give you my companionship

But my love and my friendship

Will be with you forever

II

The man who stands on the beach

Is the man who belongs to the red haired

She plays with the stones

The stones they both love and grow

They are even before God

And have his blessings

In them I find

Love is forever when it's true.

My Soul

My soul moves

Like the ocean

My souls fly

Like a bird

My soul stands

On a mountaintop

My soul swims

Like a fish

My soul is no

Teardrop

My soul is an

Ocean of feelings

My soul feels

God everywhere

My soul knows

Truth is near

My soul can't

Be change by evil

My soul can

Give others love

My soul is like

Many others

My soul is learning

To be strong

My soul has

Been searching

My soul has

Found treasures

My soul searched

And found

My soul believers

And stays alive.

Wedlock

A marriage is a holy thing

Between two individuals

Some don't respect the true

Feelings in them for one another.

What God joins together

Must not be taken apart

by any man, is said.

How come so many people

Are trying to tear those

True marriage apart?

It's hard for a woman

To find a good man

Men always want to

Do the picking first.

It's hard for a lady

to a find a friend

She might not realize

Some thinking ways of men.

A man who speaks

Many nice words

Who might not mean

Anything to him.

II

I'm not looking for

A man like that.

But a true man who loved

His lady more than that.

There is only one person who is

More precious to me than anyone else.

He has no sins and few laws

I'll always love him as a friend.

There's only one thing that's

More precious to me now

More than my life

My loving Lord who cares for us.

My true love for someone is

Who would be a best friend to me

The only man I want, well let's see,

Just have to find him first.

BLUE JEAN NORMA JEAN

Thin like tea

Calling' it blondie

Every man's fantasy

That's fine with me

She was so cute

Innocent but naughty

Still it feels funny

the thought of you

Blue jean Norma jean

Blond with style

Who made men roar

And dream of an exercise

Just with you

Only you could have

Made that effect on them

Singing shy happy birthday

Turning them all on that way

So bye, bye, Norma jean

There will only be one you

Blue jean Norma jean

We miss you.

THE CHILD DREAMS

I have a dream

That one I hope

Will come true.

I'm working on it now

It's the biggest dream

I ever had.

Life would be for filled

For it that dream

Would come true.

There might be

A change in

this world.

Can you tell me why?

Mankind is angry?

Why they fight?

Does everyone want to

Rule the world?

What are politics about?

Mirror

Have you been surprised of?

Seeing your face in the mirror?

Have you ever despised the look?

On the face you have?

Have you thought of how?

Important life can be?

Have you ever wanted?

To be free?

Have you seen the eyes of your

Believer in your mind?

Listen to the silence

Look at the birds in the sky how they fly
Look at the sea how it moves in the night
Look at the stillness in the world
Look at the houses in the dark.

Feel like the bird that lands so softly on the sea
Feel the freedom of nature in our lives
Feel the joy like the Lord over his work
Feel love for the Lord who tries.

It wasn't his fought, though my life turned out wrong
It wasn't his fought, I didn't believe
It wasn't his fought, that I couldn't give
It wasn't his will to see me sad.

Look at the birds in the sky how they fly

Look at the sea how it moves in the night

Now I love to give, live and love,

Now details seem to count a lot more

Now time seems to go away so fast

Now I feel my Lords' love for everything.

Look at the houses in the dark

Look at the ocean in the night.

The Lost love ones

To you all in pain

To you all I never get to know

How far would they have gone

Everything was going so fine

For you talented and unknown

To so many

I want to know that later

We all meet again

So goodbye all loved ones'

My friend in heart'

You're memory's stay within us

And you're reflections in our minds

Will peace be with us

For we have lost so much

We all share

That we all were

Born innocent and nice

So equal

For who are you to know

We will all meet later

When our life's are over

Life is like a holiday

Cause forever is a long time.

TRIANGLE

I

Special guests entered my friends' house

Was welcomed by good will and love

Something strange happened that night between them all

The form was built by something

I never dared to believe

the spirits assault went on

What's between you all?

What did it do?

What did it want?

You didn't abdicate

You abide your abilities to get free

Could you abolish it are they gone?

You were absent minded or absorbed on the dose

Eyes covered in pain you lived through it all.

II

I didn't want to lose you

We were anxious of its appearance

Nowhere else could I find a better friend

I never thought of an end

My mind would resemble

A naked tree, too much gone

From my small world

First-rate luck lies in your soul

It's something few of us got

I often prayed, thought I believed

In the force of God

And no life is without that

You were all joined together

In this experience

Unaimed pleasure will live when it ends.

III

I didn't leave

Something was happening

Instinct said "stay"

I witnessed the despair.

Shining star stands for happiness

Hidden demon stands for your loving soul

What is their aim?

Things may never be the same

Do they care?

The ship

The ship that sails on the waves of joy
A ship with white sails that are full of life
A ship that has no place to stay
A ship that is free like a bird in the sky.

The ship the sun shines so brightly on
The ship that doesn't know, about the anger in the world
The ship others adore
The ship that sails from now to evermore.

Near the shore it rises so proudly
Looking at the places and the faces
The faces of the flowers who love to see
How the wind of life makes the ship sail so free.

Why don't we go to the shore to see

The ship that sails to eternity

How beautiful it shines in the sunlight

As a symbol for what's best in our souls.

THE DOVE

A dove is flying on an endless flight

Towards the light

Why should I listen to people

How can they dudge me

When you can't even look out for false

Then you are just like me

The dove still flies and its closer to the light

You have to fight, fight

Nothing comes easy

You used to say that you'd win someday

But dreams like that may someday come true

So I keep on dreaming, dreaming.

FAITH

I

I'm walking in my mind

Towards a light,

I'm walking in my mind

to the sky

I'm walking in my mind

to the sun

Because you are there.

I know I have traveled

In a small circle

I know I have tried to share

My life with you

You know I want to but am I

Strong enough to

Live my life like you.

II

If you want me to go,

I will,

I will let it up to you,

what is better for me.

You have changed my life

in a short time

to something I never

Wondered could be.

You force me to

Take a risk

You know that

I can take.

G B Bernhards

If you have

A better place for me

Let me know

And I'll be on my way.

MY REPENT

Jesus forgive me

I didn't realize what I did

Until it was too late

I've got to make it all

Up to you I'm yours

I'm your child

I know you have felt

This way yourself

I will live in a prayer.

What you did to prove to me

What you did to help me

What you want me to do

Can't be much compared to

What you did and how

You have changed me.

The Way

The way I learned to live was
The way it was shown to me
The way I lived never made me happy
The way I showed it back
Was the only way I knew how.

Then you came into my life
And through your lifestyle
You taught me ways of life
I am happy with my new lifestyle
It is better than what I had before.

You talk to me of Jesus
I have heard all those words before
It took me a long while to understand
You really mean what you said
His words are your laws.

Thank you Lord

With all the thanks of all
We move to you through our souls
With all the luck of all
We move to let you all see how

Great love can be
When you know
How good love
Can be for us.

We need you Lord
We thank you for
You made our lives
So full of love.

For the children we have
For the hope we share
For peace to this world

I see you in my mind so caring

I see you in my life so sharing.

You will take us and show us

The light in our souls.

Then we have a goal to bring

Peace all over the world.

Thank you Lord

To Believe

What a fool I am and I know it
I'm nothing, what am I
I have no special assignment
I don't have any special education
I am a bad athlete
I work, I breathe, and I live,
What for, what would a stranger think?
If I would stay
" I'm a Jesus child"
" I'm just me I believe"

I feel empty, my life is changing now
And freedom will be a forgotten thing
Then I look into my baby's eyes'
And it will mean the truth to me
My flesh and blood a new person in this world
Assignment to me to care for and to help

Growing into someone, who? itself,
A personality who doesn't need anything
On the surface than its soul,
It will say proudly to the stranger
"I'm me, a Jesus child, I believe".

Christmas is Near

Candlelight and cookies
Make me feel good.
It reminds me,
That Christmas is near.
Folk forget the meaning,
Children grow up,
But they loose the feeling
What Christmas is for?

Christmas makes me feel good,
I love to give presents,
But the more I give from myself,
The more precious
Christmas is to me.
Friends seem to forget me,
Have-not heard from them
For a long time,

But I'm glad for it is Christmas.

Some lives are difficult,
Some are not,
But if we would say,
God's way, my way?
And never blame him.
I believe in Jesus,
I believe he loves me, I
believe that we will live,
In his kingdom of eternity,
He brings out the best in me.

To Dan

I I once knew a boy

Who was so kind

When he smiled it was

Like the sun that shined.

He moved away

The darkness around me

With the look of his

Dark brown eyes.

I wanted to be his girl

I saw how he cared for his flower

I knew that his girl

Would never be without love.

Time pass I lost my chance

He became a man

With the woman he loved

He had a child.

I didn't think he wouldn't
See that child,
And leave our world
So quickly, and unprepared.

II

A voice on the phone
Told me he was gone
God has taken him away
Sister's voice seemed far away.
Why should the
Lord Take him away?
Did he want him to stay
In the sky with him?
I am afraid of the lord
For he only knows
When our day will come
Will we be prepared?

His son, he never saw

Has his name,

I hope he will be kind

As he who gave him

These brown eyes.

I never forgor that boy

Whom I lost my chance for

Could he have been my only love

III

Life can die so quickly

Life can disappear

A loved one can be missed

For so many years.

An empty space in our life's

Cannot easily be replaced

Or forgotten,

Will we ever learn

To Joe

I missed what I wanted
I have lost what I needed
I have seeked for myself
And gained a peace of mind.

I know he is up there
Somewhere, I cry for him,
I know he wants to be near me
I felt his presence again.

Love to the little children love the little boy
Who wants to be
By his mother's side
Love to the mother who cries.

MY LITTLE INDIAN BOY
1973-1987

I can never forget

Those brown eyes

I can never forget

His brown hair.

I dream of him sometimes

Always smiling

I speak to him somewhere

And tell him what

I never told him when

He was still mine

I love you I miss you

I smile for you my little hero

I will never forget that smile

I can never forget his eyes

I Sometimes cry for what I have lost

I sometimes hear you comfort me

So I tell him what I should have

Told him when he was still alive

I love you I miss you

I smile to you I am your hero

I will keep on.

G.B.Bernhards.

TO BABY JOE

I will never get to know
How far you would have gone
You had everything going
Right for you.

Young talented and unknown
To so many
If I could have given you
Some time of my life.

My darling, I feel like I could have
Done a lot more
Is it not unfair to expect more
Then the best you can.

Later things seem so clear
I could have done much more

Or in another way.

But didn't notice then.

Well goodbye my darling, my friend,

Later you might see that

Your memory stays in my heart.

And I keep your reflection in my mind.

Don't worry

Don't you worry?

Close your eyes

Try to picture

A flower on the sand

Try to picture

Children on the beach

Try to rest you're acing feet.

God is watching over us now

Sending angels to every port

Every town and every farm

Try to picture him with us this time.

Angels watching everywhere

Don't try to go heaven yet

He wants us all to live happily

And when time is right

"Like naturally"

He'll send someone

Maybe not at night

Don't think of him with endless fright

We call him different names on earth

He is the one who cares for us.

You called out my name

I

I hear somebody calling
I hear somebody calling out my name
I feel somebody getting near
I feel the terror in my soul

I am afraid of the spirits
Spirits who hunt me in the dark

I close my eyes afraid of the dark
But I saw reflections in my mind
Of faces I have never seen before

They seem to be trying to tell me something
But I am too frightened to understand

I ran away from the house in the night
The wind blew angrily rain at my face

Isn't there peace in my heart
Where can I run
Desperate and full of thoughts of my condition
I called your name
I felt too much of hypocrite in me
Witch turned the words on my lips into my mind
There I stood in a silent prayer
Feeling to ashamed to ask for mercy
And too week to run
You have won and I am glad you didn't give up on me
For the road I was on only had temptations on it
I now felt the deepest pain I have ever felt
I cried out Jesus, poor Jesus

II

No longer was I afraied for myself
I felt so much pity, sympathy for the man

Who suffered to show me

I wept and shivered and my body was trembling

The fear that he felt for me

My mind was empty

I was no longer there

but I heard my soul repent to him

Poor Jesus, Jesus was I worth it

Was I there when you hung on the cross

Did I laugh, like the rest

Can you forgive me

No longer could I bear the pain

In my soul and my mind

I called out the good spirits in my heart

Asking them to comfort me someway

The door was closed

But I felt in the air

Spirits who came to humble me

Comforting me their little child

Who wanted to change its thoughts of mind

Into the philosophy of Jesus.

What do I own

Say I found out tonight

And I laughed at myself

What a dummy I have been

I gave you my soul

four years ago

I felt good after that

I gave you my life

Three years ago

I felt a bit proud

I gave you my work

Two years ago

I felt so rich

I gave you my love

One year ago

I was a hypocrite!

Now I found out tonight

I have given away

What you already had

And what you gave to me

Thank you for lending me

A body, soul, a personality

For a while Just for me.

WITH TIME

There you are in a blue dress
The kingdom is coming
Walking with all of us behind you
All together at last
We are on our way
From the darkness to the light
God there you are
Waiting for me
Watching over me
I will help while I can
And pray again
I am fine the way I am
There I am in a yellow dress
Flying in the clouds
Where did I touch the ground.

The white dove

To watch the white dove
Of peace flying high above
Brings peace to me
Brings love to me
From you to all the people
Down here on earth
Who maybe lost.

Bring peace to us
Bring love to us
And later we will be
Flying like doves In the air to bring
Peace to us
To bring faith to us.

THE STRENGTH

Your love is like

A lover's fight

Your laws are like

The words of God

You're love is like

An eternity

So dare to be

Unharmed to see

For he might arrive

To tell us story's high

To be with spiritual love

And justice for all mankind

In God we trust.

THE THOUGHT OF LIFE

So this is why

I'm a sinner

Who did try

So this is why

I'm a runner

Who went to hide

So this is why

I gained you

When I thanked you

So I thank you again

For making my life

Turn happy and bright

So I left the dark

And in the sunshine

I pray to you

I asked for a few years

Of happiness Few years of tenderness

I begged you for mercy

I asked you to look

At the years behind me

And now look at what it took

For you to prove to me

That you are willing

To make me happy

And maybe my dreams

Will come true.

So Lord I thank you

In my days

I will remain as I am

I won't try to be

Anyone else than me

But who am I?

Yours faithfully

One more believer.

THE THOUGHT OF WAITING TOO LONG

She,

With trust in you

We fear to have said

Lord to you and we

Did not really mean it.

He,

With care for her and

With fear to loose her

She is a lady who beliefs

I will remember her

She,

Love will keep me warm

In the cold nights

Holding my love ones'

In my mind

Without fearing the time.

He,

You look at the northern lights

You are there far away

The time will come, child.

She,

I am waiting to go to him

Time will come

Then I will join him

Hope I will be ready.

The Shadow

I

O Lord take one look at me

You'll see a shadow over me

High above me, hiding me

O Lord take one look at me

High above you'll see

The shadow over me

Once was low and covered my soul

I pray to thee

I pray to thee

Please take it away

Make me here to stay

Help me to be

A child to thee

Let the shadow fly
So high away from me
Now I look at thee
In the heavens
No shadow hanging over me

You took one look at me
You saw a shadow covered me

II

I pray to thee
I pray to thee

I was running from myself
Had no one to care for
And no one to help
The size of us all

Lord forgive me now

I know you understand

I don't have to fight

You will fight for me

I hope so, so you will never loose me

I believe that fighting

Among men is all wrong

We don't have to fight at all

Let there be peace on earth

Forever and ever now

Let there be understanding

Love for every human being

We all believe in someone

What we might believe

We don't always admit

To ourselves nor tell others

For we are so small

III

Life is sometimes crazy

You look into your eyes

You wonder if you were still hole

Life is sometimes wonderful

You look into your eyes

You wonder why they smile

Life is up and down

Time floats away

My time might take a while

Will I ever be happy

Will I ever live again

Will I ever be forgiven

Lord you know my soul

You are the truth in my life

I hope I can keep the laws

I am a week one

Afraid of something

Please give me strength

Please forgive my soul.

THE SOUNDS OF THE SOULS

God loves us all

He would want us to know

That he wants to help us

He would want us to be his children

Of the world in spirit and in life

Let sing a song for him

And ask in our hearts

We wonder is he real

Why don't we see him

Does he see me

Does he hear me

We keep on wondering

We have music in the air

From land to land

Why do we wonder if

God and his heaven

Can not find our tone and

messages from our souls.

THE PAIN OF LOVE

Sometimes I can live

Without a fright

Sometimes I can look

Into the night.

When you will die

You will see

Heaven in the sky

Through the sign that we gave him

To brighten up the spiritual world

So we will learn why

That God gave us

The life within

That God gave us

The love in the beginning

That God gave us

The freedom to believe.

Please have patience for me

I have this dream to be
Able to live forever
Please have love for me

For I have this caring
Hidden inside me
Are we sure they will live too

Those who tempt and judge me
For they lie and make life hard for me
So I want to see

The life in heaven
Those nice faces
Good places

To be able to understand
The key for happiness
And the cure for life.

THE PRESSURE

Lord you gave us your life And your love You are the blessed one

So don't be angry

With me Lord

For I have this dream

To call out your name

Jesus, Jesus

You are the only light

That is true

The glory is yours

I love you Lord

Don't misunderstand me

I want to let people know

I believe in you

Jesus, dear Jesus

I don't need a sign

To believe in you

I feel when I pray

You're near my soul

Therefore I need to know

This dream who hunted me

Who would not let me be free

Until I had made this song

So glory to you all

Who want to hear

Glory to you all

Also those who fear

For he is with us

Till the end

With belief in him and with his forgiveness

May we up rise towards the light.

The sailor

My heart is heavy with

The soil I carry

Away for his grave

I felt like I had failed

A tall man with hair

Like fire

Young and strong

I felt death approach him.

The sea took you away

Took you from your love

Took you away

From us all.

I was afraid that

My dream of him

That he would die

Would not be a lie.

He worked at sea

Then one day he did

A heroic thing and now

He doesn't breathe anymore.

The Injuries

You are special to me

Your existence cures me

So please have patience for me

The spark is still in me

I try to hold on to my forgiveness

That I will be as long as I believe

It would be difficult to be

A trembling leaf flying in the wind

Afraid to be nothing

Afraid to be something

Cause with time you see yourself

In another way

Who is afraid to get hurt again.

I love you Lord

So don't give up on me

I need you Lord
So don't be angry with me

I worship you and all
You're glory
I long to be able to
Tell you
The history of me and
About my mistakes

I want you to be kind
Like I were a baby girl
I want you to beware
Of love and the pain that is
Hidden inside of me.

The Innocence

I see in my mind

You're caring

I feel you in my life

So I'm fearing

I have forgotten

All the wrong that

I have done

The way I live then

I want you back into my life

My hope for a life is with my love

But my love will not know

For he might be like other men.

THE MISSIONARY

I saw myself standing
On a stage
I was amazed by
Myself singing

Singing to people
About God, love,
And life
Proud to be there

I said: God take my share
I want to hunt down souls
With broken hearts
And sing to them about love.

So they would
Stop crying, stop dyeing,

And sign them over

To my God.

I wondered:

Am I supposed to turn

Them to Christ

Am I supposed to save them

Through Christ

Die to let them just feel

That love is within and

God is more than a man

He is

Love for all humanity

No matter how we might pray.

What kind of life we might be

Life is like the only thing we are

And the only thing we lose for

Then there is no use for anything else.

THE CAT

My cat was black
I love her more than
Mother loved her flowers

My black cat is
Dying tonight
I lay by her side
I am warm and sweating
She is cold and dry

I hope gran will take care
Of her after she dies

They say that animals
Don't have souls
Only instinct
But I need her
I feel lonely without her

Sometimes wonder why

It is like she understands me

I hope I was not too strict to her

In her short life.

MOTHER DEAR MOTHER

I know your mother and I
Could have been good friends
I am sorry she's gone but still I am
I get to know a part of her through you

She is in the spiritual world
Maybe she is watching over us
Waiting for our child
For she cares for our life's

I hope your father will like me
Hope he will be nice to me
For I am stubborn and shy
And maybe wouldn't talk first

The beginning could be difficult
But that cannot change us
The rest might be more difficult
But we would stay happy.

Farewell to my father

I will let the memories of

Our best days be with me

To let no negativity

Darken my mind

When I said farewell to my father

I saw pictures of us

All the best days we have had

I could see now H

ow glad I was to remember

So farewell to my father

You showed me more caring

Then any other person I have known

For you did your best

To stand by me

Through mostly all my life

You were there for me

You helped me more

Than anyone else.

For my children

It was for love

Send from my soul

Too my children

To be far away

but still near

For I had a place in my heart.

Was my life with you

When I said I believe

Did you send a soul to my child

When I asked you please.

For he is so wonderful

So bright and kind

Shorth to his smile

And good in his mind.

I have asked you also for
A place in your heart
For my brown haired body
He is so smart and so tall.

I'm sure you love my baby boy
With his black hair and blue eyes
Modest he is and shy
They all remind me of the boy I once had.

He was their brother with big brown eyes
I miss him now as ever for he has left
You take care of him for me.

I have asked you also for
A place in your heart, so take care
We send him our love.

We miss him too but
Later we will hopefully
All meet again.

Thought of God

I

Think of God as a person
Not the scary father
Not the strict mother
But as the best parent
That always loves you

Think of all of us as equal
He gives us all a spirit, a soul,
Then we are on our own
Nature takes it course
Reality is another dimension

Think of God as love
Who has overcome
All anger, hate, and other moods
There is justice for all

We should not blame him

Think how we are slow

Accusing him for things

That nature and reality

Does to our lives God is only love

Who are we to say

That he is on our side

When we are fighting,

He's hopeful we will see

There is no separation

II

We must understand

That laws that men

Have been writing

Are their words to share

Do we really care

Of others in their situations

Will we ever learn

Evil is not out there
Just stupidity and fanatics
Who wash away reason and sensibility
When we think we know it all
We have closed our mind to God

We cannot resemble us to him
Use signs and laws to dominate
The civilizations for mankind
When will we learn we are equal
God as a person is to understand
Our souls are all children to him

We take away from others
All love and teach each other hate
And stupid laws that separate us all
We are so far away to realize
God is not mankind
For he is a person who understands us all
Not like us in our deceiving ways
God helps us all no matter what way we pray
For all we do say remember me that day
Now I have said it all.

www.ingramcontent.com/pod-product-compliance
Lightning Source LLC
Chambersburg PA
CBHW071430070526
44578CB00001B/54